Hidden

Other books from Strength to Stand

The Complete Evangelism Guidebook

Hidden

A 40-DAY JOURNEY

OF KNOWING CHRIST AND MAKING HIM KNOWN

SCOTT DAWSON

Birmingham, Alabama

Strength to Stand Publishing in Association with
Life Bible Study
100 Missionary Ridge
Birmingham, AL 35242
Life Bible Study is an imprint of Iron Stream Media
IronStreamMedia.com

ISBN-13: 978-1-56309-412-5
Ebook ISBN: 978-1-59669-070-7

1 2 3 4 5—23 22 21 20 19

TABLE OF CONTENTS

ACKNOWLEDGMENTS

I once heard John Maxwell say something like, "A self-made man certainly never makes much." That statement has never been more true concerning this book. This achievement has been accomplished by a team.

Thank you to John Herring and the entire staff at Iron Stream Media. John is the epitome of a true professional. Thank you to Kim Beverage, my assistant, who provided the blocks in the schedule for this to be possible. She is my right arm (and left) in getting so many things accomplished in ministry.

A personal thank you to Amber Hardy, my research assistant, who did most of the work for this book. Amber is a bright, rising leader in ministry. She does not know the word *can't* and will work tirelessly to reach every deadline. Amber, *thank you!*

This forty-day journey has been made profoundly better by every individual writer that contributed. These devotionals are written from multiple unique perspectives, including youth pastors, ministry staff members, former interns, spouses, and volunteers at our conferences. This book is also fortunate to include a student contributor, who submitted her writing in faith during our student writing competition. Thank you, Lindsey Wood, for your contribution!

To all of our contributors, I would like to thank you for giving this project your time and prayer. Thank you for being faithful enough to proclaim the life-changing words of the Bible and vulnerable enough to share how these words have impacted you personally.

Finally, thank you, Tarra. She is rock solid and my perfect helpmate. I am so thankful the Lord brought us together. To Christ and Him alone be all glory and praise for what He has done!

Introduction to Hidden

A 40-Day Journey
of Knowing Christ
and Making Him Known

It is truly a holy paradox, the idea that each of us tries to hide from God. However, Scripture teaches us we cannot hide from God. If I dig a pit, He is there. Since the Garden of Eden, humankind has tried to hide. For thousands of years, nothing has really ever changed. When faced with the shame of our sin, we hide from God.

The paradox is that someone can actually be hidden in Christ. Paul says, in Colossians 3:3, "For you died, and your life is now hidden with Christ in God." Think about it like this: when you come to know Christ, He engulfs you. He surrounds you. Sustains you. Empowers you. As God sees you, He sees you in Christ, perfect. It is no longer attempting to hide from God but to be in right relationship with Him.

There is no longer shame but rather forgiveness. Shame is the end result of being lost in sin. Of knowing you have done something wrong, but being unable to find out how to make it right. Let's face it. We are guilty. No doubt about it. No one forces us to sin; it just comes naturally. However, Christ makes us complete. He forgives and cleanses. First John 1:9 says, "If we confess our sins, he is faithful and just and will forgive us our sins and purify us from *all* unrighteousness" (emphasis added). To be hidden in Christ means no more shame for the covered and uncovered sin in my life!

When we are hidden in Christ we are no longer hiding in sin but rather walking in the power of the Spirit. Have you ever been in a difficult situation and tried to do something to get out of it, only to make it worse? Then you keep doing things to make the situation worse and worse until, finally, you just want to give up? That is our sin nature. Sin makes us do things that damage us more than we can imagine. In Christ, we are able to walk in victory. Again, please do not think Christ doesn't have power over sin. He does. So many Christians want to justify their sin while excusing it and indulging it. Don't do that! Christ has victory over the grave. Sin has no dominion over a follower of Christ!

When we are hidden in Christ, we are no longer disguised by insecurity but live in boldness. Confidence is not walking into the room thinking you are better than everyone but walking into a room and not comparing yourself to anyone. If ever we needed a generation of bold believers— it is now. The most insecure people I have met hide it in a form of arrogance. There is a major difference between arrogance and confidence. Arrogance is thinking you are better than anyone. Confidence means you are secure in who you are.

What would it be like in your life if you lived by these three stark differences—to have forgiveness, walk in power, and live in a Holy boldness? Think about this opportunity over this forty-day journey. This is your opportunity to experience a true transformation. These days will bring inspiration, challenge, and opportunities. Everyone is hidden—it only depends where you place your trust. In yourself or in Christ. Now, come on . . . let's get started!

Seek

Day 1

INTRODUCTION TO SEEK

So many Christians have misunderstood the Christian walk as one that does not seek after God.

If you went to a restaurant for a meal and never got seated, never was waited on, and had no one attending to your needs, would you have ever eaten? No. Our relationship with God is similar. When we do not seek Him and search for His wisdom, we miss out on the opportunity to know the Almighty God. How can we know him better? By seeking His will and serving His purposes.

Isaiah 40:31 (NKJV) says, "Those who wait on the LORD shall renew their strength." The word for *renew* can be best translated, "exchange." Did you catch that? If we wait upon the Lord, just like a waitress or waiter in a restaurant, we will exchange our strength for God's strength. His joy for ours. Does God have enough strength? Wisdom? Joy? As we seek after Him, we realize He provides all we have ever needed.

Jesus tells us to "seek first his kingdom and his righteousness, and all these things will given to you as well" (Matthew 6:33). What does that mean to you? Quite simply, pursue Him. Live life in light of eternity. I am not suggesting you quit sports, forget studying, or never get married. Rather you should submit everything else to His authority. It will make life so much better. Trust me.

To borrow the Westminster Shorter Catechism, "A man's chief end is to glorify God, *and* enjoy Him forever." When you pursue Him, you ultimately find joy. You find peace. You find purpose. People live for items that simply will never satisfy. Don't become one of those perilous pursuit people. Discover purpose. This happens when you find life!

Are you seeking after the true God in order to serve Him, or are you creating a God that serves your sinful purposes? This may mean you will need to rearrange some priorities or your schedule, and in your pursuit, discover the purpose of life!

Day 2

God did this so that they would seek him and perhaps reach out for him and find him, though he is not far from any one of us.

—Acts 17:27

In my twenty-five years of being a student pastor, the topic of how to find God's will for our lives has been one of the most frequently asked questions. Most everyone wants to discover what God wants them to do and fulfill what He created us to do. God's will is His purpose for our lives, and to find His will, we must first find Him.

Questioning how to know God's will has kind of gotten a bad reputation over the years. Many think it is some mysterious thing God is trying to hide from us. In reality, if you are seeking a close relationship to Jesus, God's will usually isn't too hard to find. Why? Because a relationship with Jesus *is* a relationship with God! Acts 17:27 says, "He is not far from any one of us."

You see, God's will is really more like playing hide and seek with my youngest son Benjamin (when he was little). If we ever had a little trouble finding him, all we would have to do is sing the first part of the Dora the Explorer cartoon song, and he would stand up and sing the rest of it.

Us: "Dora Dora Dora"
Benjamin (standing up): "The Explorer!"

Benjamin announced his location with a song, and he stood up making himself clearly visible. That's exactly how God wants us to feel when we are seeking to discover His will for our lives!

However, finding God's will may not be as easy as we wish because we are too often trying to discover *our* will instead of *His* will. When we look for our will, we find destruction. But when we seek the Lord's will, it leads us to life in Him. Let's be perfectly clear . . . God's will is always better than our will! That's why He makes finding His will easy. He's not keeping it a secret. He has purpose and plans for those He loves.

Jeremiah 29:13 says, "You will seek me and find me when you seek me with all your heart." Seek God, and you will find Him!

Have you been called by God to serve in any specific area of the church?

Where can we learn the most about who God is and His purpose for our life?

What does Acts 17:27 mean to you?

Day 3

But from there you will seek the LORD your God and you will find him, if you search after him with all your heart and with all your soul. When you are in tribulation, and all these things come upon you in the latter days, you will return to the LORD your God and obey his voice. For the LORD your God is a merciful God. He will not leave you or destroy you or forget the covenant with your fathers that he swore to them.

—Deuteronomy 4:29–31 ESV

The definition of *seek* is the attempt or desire to obtain or achieve something.

In life we're constantly seeking something—popularity, acceptance, a new job, wealth, or a relationship. We seek these things to fill a void in our life, but when these things only partially fill the void, we move onto the next thing to try to fill it. The world tries to offer everything it can to fill the empty place in our heart, and a few of these things may work temporarily, but nothing seems to last.

Think about something you're seeking right now. What is it, and is it going to matter in a month, a year, or even five years?

We all go through life seeking things, but are these things going to matter in the long run? We often find ourselves seeking after things that only last for a season instead of seeking the one who can fill the void in our heart for eternity and is constant—God.

Deuteronomy 4:29–31 talks about how seeking God with our whole hearts leads us to find Him and that He will reveal himself to us. Whether it's a time of joy or trial, God is there with mercy if we are willing to seek after Him instead of trying to fix things in our own power. Worldly things end. Jobs are lost, relationships end, money runs out, friends leave, but God is constant and will not leave us. He desires to have a relationship with us that glorifies Him and shares His love with the people around us.

Seek the Lord, and rest in Him!

What have you been seeking that hasn't filled "the void"?

How can we continually seek the Lord?

What does Deuteronomy 4:29–31 mean to you?

Day 4

Draw near to God, and he will draw near to you.
Cleanse your hands, you sinners, and purify your
hearts, you double-minded.

—James 4:8 ESV

When was the last time you played hide-and-seek? Last week? Last year? Sometime in the last decade? No matter how long it's been, I guarantee you remember how to play. In the traditional game, there are many hiders and usually one seeker. It is the seeker's job to find the hiders. Depending on how well each hider is hidden, the game can stretch on or end very quickly. But in every good game of hide-and-seek, there is that last person who has yet to be found because their spot is just too good. You know the type—the no-sound-while-breathing-hiding-in-the-off-limits-spot friend who only reveals their location when they are certain you have tried everything and searched everywhere. They leave their hiding spot with cries of "I won, I won," and everyone groans and then you play another round with the goal of finding them first next time! In the end, though, it's just a game.

A lot of times I think we view our relationship with God as a game of hide-and-seek in which you are the seeker and God is the champion hider. And perhaps it can feel like that when we can't visibly see or audibly hear Him. But God is not one to hide from His children. He does not watch us from His secret spot, giggling that we haven't found Him yet. He doesn't reveal His hiding place with a grand announcement that makes us feel slightly silly. To put it plainly, God does not play games with us. Scripture very clearly says what God does when we seek Him out.

James 4:8 says, "Draw near to God, and he *will* draw near to you" (emphasis added). That means when we seek the Lord out, He actually *comes closer* to us. The God of the universe, who set the stars in motion and breathed breath into your lungs, comes close to you! Notice that it's not a suggestion but a command. "Draw near." There is no asking here because God knows His presence is the best thing for us. And did you catch that word *will?* That's not a *might* or *maybe* or *if He feels like it*. It's a promise. And we know from God's Word that He keeps His promises. He promised to make Abraham a great nation, and *He did*. He promised to deliver the Israelites from Egypt, and *He did*. He promised to send a Redeemer who would take away the sins of the world, and *He did*. There are so many examples throughout Scripture of God keeping His promises—what makes us think this would be any different?

The next time you feel discouraged in your walk with the Lord, remember the promise of James 4:8—when you seek Him, He will come near to you.

How would you counsel a friend who is seeking God?

What are some ways we can avoid seeking false gods?

What does James 4:8 mean to you?

Doubt

Day 5

INTRODUCTION TO DOUBT

She was quick to speak and determined in her inflection. "I doubt God." It was the first time I had heard this young lady be so conflicted in her personal spiritual nature. She confessed it made her feel bad to acknowledge, but she couldn't go on in this turmoil. She was not denying God, only doubting Him.

You may have experienced the same emotion at some point in your life. If not, you may in the future. Allow me to give you some comfort. There is a major difference between doubt and unbelief. There are a multitude of Scripture passages that speak against doubt, fear, and unbelief. Unbelief is when you are not open to the concept of a personal God. Even worse, you have convinced yourself there is no God. How does one get to that point in his or her life?

To say there is no God means you are the supreme knowledge of the universe. So, if you are reading this and are in that situation, I have only one phrase for you, "God help you!" Why? Because I do not care how many tests you passed or YouTube videos you have watched, you can't have all the knowledge of the universe. Not even close. To remove even the remote possibility of a living God shows the extent of your arrogance and need for repentance. Sorry, bud, you just aren't that sharp.

Now, you may be reading this and saying, "Scott, I am not saying there isn't a God, but I sometimes doubt it." We can work with this! Doubt is the one item we all struggle with from time to time. So what are we to do with doubt? One thing we do is not let it keep us down. Don't do it. Stand up to your doubt.

First, realize you don't know everything. This is not to suggest we do not study, pursue knowledge, or relish in ignorance. It is to admit our humanity. We simply do not know everything. Second, we focus on the fundamentals. Don't spend time on the peripheral issues, but instead focus on the fundamentals of your faith. The evidence is overwhelming of the existence of God, the authority of Scripture, and the validity of the resurrection. This gives you wind back in your sails.

Third, check the pulse for your doubt. Where did it come from? What gave it life in your life, and does it revolve around a person, an influence, or sin? This gives you the perspective of who is actually helping or hurting you. Fourth, ask God to use it for your good. Doubt can lead you into a deeper understanding of faith and trust. Don't let is paralyze your faith; let it deepen your faith. Over these next three days you will learn the prize of winning the battle over doubt. Come on . . . don't have doubt in it . . . walk through it!

Day 6

"'If you can'?" said Jesus. "Everything is possible for one who believes." Immediately the boy's father exclaimed, "I do believe; help me overcome my unbelief!"

—Mark 9:23–24

Have you ever felt as though you were neck-deep in a situation that was much greater than you? Have you ever felt as though you have tried every possible solution yet found none? Have you ever felt as though your prayers hit the ceiling, and God was nowhere to be found? It is in these moments of darkness when we often find ourselves in the shroud of doubt. We wonder where God is, what is happening, and what the heck is going on.

Mark 9 introduces us to a man who was in a shroud of doubt. His son had been having a medical issue where he would fall to the ground, have a seizure, and foam at the mouth. The medical condition was clearly affecting the boy's life and caused hurt for the family. The dad had tried everything, yet the seizures continued. As the man approached Jesus, he explained the plight of the boy and asked if Jesus could please help his son.

In Mark 9:23–24 we pick up the exchange between Jesus and the dad. Jesus affirms He is one who can do anything for those who believe. The father responds just as Jesus got the final words out of His mouth: "I do believe; help me overcome my unbelief." The dad affirms he knows Jesus is who He says He is and can do what He says He can do while also seeking Jesus to give him additional faith to believe.

When you find yourself in the darkness of doubt, there are some truths to remember. First, remember that who Jesus says He is and what Jesus says that He can do does not change based on your circumstance. Jesus is stable. Jesus is sure. Jesus is reliable. You can depend on Him. Second, remember Jesus wants to give you strength and the faith to believe.

Today, you are either walking around in a shroud of doubt or there are people around you walking in one. If you are in the dark, cling to who Jesus is, and let Him be your strength. If you know someone in the dark, encourage them with who Jesus is, and point them to seek God for belief even in the darkness.

Where in your life have you hesitantly asked for help from the Lord? Do you remember the faith it took?

What does it mean to say God is the author of our faith?

What does Mark 9:23–24 mean to you?

And without faith it is impossible to please Him,
for he who comes to God must believe that He is,
and that He is a rewarder of those who seek Him.

—Hebrews 11:6 NASB

The Cambridge dictionary definition of doubt is (a feeling of) not being certain about something, especially about how good or true it is. It is the very first thing Satan used in the garden to cause man to sin against God. It is still one of Satan's most-used weapons to cause humankind to sin against God today.

In Genesis 3, doubt caused at least four things to happen. It caused Eve and Adam to question the truth of God's Word. In Genesis 3:1, Satan asked the question, "Has God said?" (NASB). In verse 4 Satan completely denied God's Word, saying, "You surely will not die!" (NASB).

It caused them to question the goodness of God. In verses 2–3 they asked why they could eat from of all the trees in the garden but not from the one in the middle of the garden. Why not that one? Because God said, "You shall not eat from it or touch it, or you will die" (v. 3 NASB).

It caused them to desire to be like God or to be God. In verse 4 Satan says, "God knows that in the day you eat from it your eyes will be opened, and you will be like God"

(NASB). Verse 6 says, "When the woman saw that the tree was good for food, and that it was a delight to the eyes, and that the tree was desirable to make one wise" (NASB). She may as well have said, "I want to make my own decisions. I don't want anyone to tell me what to do."

It caused them to disobey God. Verse 6 says, "She took from its fruit and ate; and she gave also to her husband with her, and he ate" (NASB).

Doubt unchecked by faith will ultimately bring one to either ignore God's Word or to totally reject it. The result is sin. Someone has said, "Sin always takes you farther than you want to go, keeps you longer than you want to stay, and makes you pay more than you want to pay."

As in these verses, doubt always costs something.

It cost Adam and Eve the peace of God's presence. Verse 8 says they hid themselves from the presence of the Lord God among the trees of the garden.

It cost them the plenty of God's provision. Read verses 17–19. Verse 19 says, "By the sweat of your face you will eat bread, till you return to the ground" (NASB).

The only way to overcome doubt is by exercising faith. Psalm 119:11 says, "I have hidden your word in my heart that I might not sin against you."

Why is it important to understand doubt as a feeling of uncertainty?

How can doubt lead to sin if not combated with God's truth?

What does Genesis 3:1–24 mean to you?

Day 8

The LORD is good. A *stronghold* in the day of trouble; and He knows those who trust in Him.

—Nahum 1:7 NKJV (emphasis added)

Doubt. Most of us have probably had a bit of experience with doubt in our lives, am I right? Whether it's doubting that your mom's food is going to be good, or doubting that your dad actually knows where he's going in the car—we've all run into it before.

We doubt Jesus all the time. Don't say you never have—because you have! Through every decision, every hesitation, you've questioned Him at least once. Well, you're not the only one, that's for sure. One of Jesus' disciples is actually nicknamed *Doubting* Thomas!

Take a look at John 20:24–29 in your Bible. If you had seen Jesus as the disciples had, wouldn't you run and tell your friends? Yes! Of course! Ten of Jesus' disciples did just that—they ran and told Thomas they had seen Jesus. They told him they had seen His hands and His side. In verse 25 Thomas tells them, "Unless I see the nail marks in his hands and put my finger where the nails were, and put my hand to his side, I will not believe."

Now, if I was in this situation, I probably wouldn't have been too patient with Thomas. I might've just waved my hands in his face and said, "Bro . . . this is Jesus . . . *Je-sus*. Ya know, born of a virgin, miracle worker . . . any of this ringing a bell? He's *here*." But God's timing is always perfect. We see in verse 26 that after some time had passed, Jesus appeared to them again, only this time Thomas was there. Jesus came in and told Thomas to *stop* doubting and *believe*.

It is so important to remember this simple fact: Jesus did not rebuke Thomas for his *doubts*. He rebuked him for his *unbelief*. Jesus wants us to be confident in His greatness even when we are feeling discouraged and defeated (and in this world, that might be a lot). I know it's not easy—I don't think it ever will be easy.

My dad reminded me a while back that when you're feeling doubt, discouragement, and defeat you should always keep your eyes on the finish line and *remember* God's promises for you. Nahum 1:7 (NKJV) tells us, "The LORD is good. a *stronghold* in the day of trouble; and He knows those who trust in Him" (emphasis added). *Remember* that it's all for His glory.

Are you currently going through something that's causing you to doubt, or even not believe, like Thomas? I just have one simple favor to ask of you.

I want you to write a short prayer, first asking God to forgive you for any unbelief you've had, and then asking Him to give you the strength and courage each day to keep your focus completely and undoubtedly on Him.

> What are some of your biggest doubts, and have any of them turned into unbelief?
>
> How can you help others fight doubt and trust in God?
>
> What does Nahum 1:7 mean to you?

Lost

Day 9

INTRODUCTION TO LOST

No one gets lost on purpose. It just happens. It has happened to me and probably to you. Once on a trip we decided to take a shortcut. Three hours later, we were lost. I do not mean misplaced, I mean *lost*. There was no hope. Well, that's what I was thinking. Finally, we retraced our turns to find a familiar place, and we were back on track.

No one gets lost on purpose. This is also true in our life journeys. No one purposely wants to get lost on their journey. If you find yourself lost, what can you do? First, just stop. Take a breath. Don't continue to go any further until you get perspective. It is true you cannot change yesterday, but the good news is you can change the tomorrows. So stop. Second, review your steps. How did you get here? What decisions were rushed into or made from emotion? This will give you your map.

Third, who is looking for you and who isn't? This is a reality check. Many of the people we think of as friends are only acquaintances. They are present in the fun times, but if we were lost, they would not search for us. The Good Shepherd will leave the ninety-nine safe sheep to find the one that is lost. He is passionately pursuing you. Fourth, turn around. The biblical word for this is *repent*. Repentance is simply turning your direction. I am going this way and thinking this way, acting this way—but then I turn my thoughts and actions in another other direction.

Repentance is the key to being found. You can't just think about it; you have to do it. Bring it to action. Most people live their life from "almost to almost." Let's not be an almost generation. Let's live life from a new perspective.

Allow me to explain. Without repentance, you will want to keep trying, attempting to be found without any regard to what God has in store for you. To use a business illustration, you will want to go from good to great. You can do this without repentance. However God doesn't call us to be great but rather to be the best. It is God's best that is His desire for you. This comes by realizing when we are lost, recognizing what got us lost, realizing He is searching for us, and repenting so He can show us the way back to Himself and His safety.

Day 10

For the Son of Man came to seek and to save the lost.

—Luke 19:10

Lost. It's a feeling we've all had but one we never get used to. You've probably had the feeling as you sat in the middle of algebra class and wondered, "Who thought it would be a good idea to add letters to math?" As horrible as may be to feel lost in a single moment, it is an even worse feeling to be lost as you live your daily life.

The feeling of being lost can quickly overtake you, even as you try so hard to fulfill your life with things this world says are supposed to make us whole or give us purpose. You quickly realize, though, that all of the relationships you build, all of the trophies you earn, and all of the fame and fortune you acquire through this world still leaves you feeling one way—*lost*. In Luke 19 we see a man who has encountered this same experience. By the world's standards, he should have been the most content and satisfied person on the planet, but he wasn't. Today, trust in these truths from the story of Zacchaeus.

First, God provides. Many of us are providers. We provide for ourselves, our families, and our friends. Sadly, we often miss out on how God provides for us. Monetarily, Zacchaeus did not need anyone to provide for him. He had everything he could have ever wanted. Yet we see that as he approached Jesus, he had a sudden realization of how inadequate his resources were compared to the Son of God. In that moment, God provided the exact thing Zacchaeus needed to see Jesus—a tree. It is beautiful how such a small, insignificant object can still bring us to God. You may feel lost today, but remember you serve a God who will provide you with all you could ever need.

Second, God pays attention. In the hustle and bustle of this life, it is easy to think you are forgotten and lost in the background of billions of other people. Don't forget God pays attention to you! In the middle of the busy crowd, *Jesus paid attention* to Zacchaeus. He saw him and his need, and He reached out to him. God has not forgotten you. While you might feel as though you have lost Him, He has not lost you! God pays attention to your life!

Last, God proves His love. We don't serve a God who claims to love us yet doesn't back it up with actions! Luke 19:10 says, "The Son of Man came to seek and save the lost." That truth is for me, and that truth is for you! God proves His love for you as He actively and passionately seeks you! You may feel lost today, but remember, God is waiting to prove His love to you!

In what ways does the world contribute to feelings of being lost?

Thinking of Zacchaeus and the tree that God provided for him, what are some ways God has used ordinary things to bring you back to Him?

What does Luke 19:10 mean to you?

Day 11

For the LORD will not forsake his people; he will
not abandon his heritage; for justice will return
to the righteous, and all the upright in heart will
follow it.

—Psalm 94:14–15 ESV

Do you remember being a young child and losing your
mom in the grocery store? Your heart racing, tears
welling up in your eyes, feeling as though you have lost your
mom forever? The feeling was dreadful!

This is something believers have experienced many
times in their walk with Jesus. Imagine the grocery store
experience as your life. You are doing great. You're walking with Jesus, speaking kind words, praying, reading your
Bible, buying all the spiritual vegetables you need in order
to further your relationship with Christ and live a life that is
pleasing to Him. And then you see it—the candy aisle. You
see the bright packaging and the fun shapes of the sweet
treats. You can't help but walk over. You leave Jesus' side
for just one second to indulge yourself in the seemingly
sweet temptation, and then poof. He's out of sight.

Sadly, we may not have the same reaction we had as
children when we lost our way in the grocery store as we
do in our spiritual life. We allow that one indulgence to lead

to another and another—and then we find ourselves feeling too far away from Jesus to ever go back. Remember feeling this way as a child? Feeling so far away from your mom that you may never find her again? In that moment, the most beautiful and relieving thing is when your mom turned out to be just right around the corner, knowing right where you were the whole time.

In your walk with God, you might lose your way. You will venture into a place where you feel that it's okay to do life on your own until you realize you've traded the beauty of Christ for the fleeting pleasures of the world. This is when you finally admit defeat. This is when you call out for help. Psalm 94:14–15 says: "For the LORD will not forsake his people; he will not abandon his heritage; for justice will return to the righteous, and all the upright in heart will follow it."

Lost does not mean forgotten; lost does not mean forsaken. Lost means you can be found. And when you call out for help, Jesus is never too far away. He's been keeping an eye on you this whole time, waiting for you to run back to Him.

What does it mean that the Lord will not forsake His people?

How can you avoid following the path of the lost?

What does Psalm 94:14–15 mean to you?

Day 12

But while he was still a long way off, his father saw him and was filled with compassion for him; he ran to his son, threw his arms around him and kissed him.

—Luke 15:20

The parable of the lost son, found in Luke 15:11–32, begins with a beloved son approaching his gracious father. Instead of returning love to his father, he requests his inheritance in advance—a request that implied to his father that he preferred everything his father's wealth could afford him as opposed to a personal relationship with him. Despite the fact he didn't owe his son anything, the father graciously granted the son's request and gifted him his inheritance.

Unsurprisingly, the impulsive and immature son took the father's fortune and left the father's property, heading out into the world in pursuit of all the earthly pleasures his newfound fortune could afford him. He lived like a king for a season, denying himself nothing, indulging himself in every way, and losing himself in his quest to satisfy his appetites. He squandered the money and ended up in the pigsty—literally sharing food with animals.

It was there he hit rock bottom and had a moment of realization. He remembered the goodness of his father and the life he once enjoyed. He decided to return home and beg his father to take him back in as a servant. He didn't realize he had greatly underestimated his father and his deep love and overwhelming grace. He returned home prepared to propose a transactional relationship, arriving home only to find his father already running toward him to embrace him! He had prepared himself to be a servant to an employer, but he found himself restored as a beloved son to a gracious father that day.

So often we find ourselves in similar moments of repentance—looking around and realizing just how far we've wandered from our Heavenly Father. We realize how we've taken the grace he's given us and squandered it on ourselves in our pursuit of happiness and satisfaction outside of Him. It's in those moments we have a choice to make. Will we return as sons and daughters or as servants? Will we humbly return to our Father, confident of His compassion and love, ready to walk in the grace He offers? Or will we choose the hamster wheel of empty religion—choosing instead to propose to God a transactional relationship based upon our performance and what we can "bring to the table" as mere servants? Your Heavenly Father is looking to restore you as a beloved child! Take Him up on His amazing grace and walk into this new life confident of His love and approval.

Have you ever experienced this kind of spiritual clarity—when you realized you'd squandered God's grace in pursuit of life outside of Him and recognized you were lost and needed to "go back home"?

After recognizing your need for repentance, do you tend to move forward in confidence of God's love and grace toward you or do you tend to feel the need to "work for God" in order to regain His approval?

What does the parable of the prodigal son mean to you?

Identity

Day 13

Introduction to Identity

It seems every Bible study, conference, and Instagram post today focuses on identity. Some steal your identity, others try to define your identity, but most have never discovered your true identity. *Identity* is defined as the fact of being who or what a person or thing is. Notice the term *fact*. Most people think of their identity by feelings and not fact.

Basing your decisions on feeling is never a good idea. Feelings are like your pulse. Your pulse goes up and down based on distinct situations. If you are stressed, tired, fearful, or any other emotion, your pulse will skyrocket. To make a decision of your identity based on an emotional situation is dangerous. You cannot base it on how you feel at the time or base it on what others say about you. It must be built on truth.

Truth can be compared to a muscle. Your muscle is always consistent. It is not altered by how you feel or by a certain emotional moment. Listen to me, there is truth in this world. It may not be taught in school or concerned by society, but truth is the only way to get a grasp of your identity.

So if we desire to know our identity, what is the truth that you can accept? First, we are flawed. That doesn't sound nice, but it is true. However, you are not alone. We are *all* flawed. Every one of us. No exemptions. Second, we are loved. The deepest desire of a human is to be loved. You are loved by God. Third, you are choosing your own identity. You are either accepting the label by others or you are searching for who you really are. It is your choice. Either be a pinball bouncing from one opinion to another or believe the following characteristics from Scripture that have been consistent for thousands of years!

Now, in order to truly know who you are, you have to know the one who gives you your identity. You have to know God. Know Him through Jesus who died on the Cross for your sin. He arose. No one has ever done that to never die again . . . only Jesus. So, if you know Him, you will relish what He says about you.

You are a child of God. The one who has no beginning or end. You are a joint heir of the kingdom of God. You are an ambassador. When you speak, you represent the kingdom of God. (Remember that!) Ephesians 2:10 says you are a work of art, Philippians 3:20 says you are a citizen of heaven, and Romans 5:8 says we are greatly loved. When you know who you are, you will not wonder what others think you are. Walk today knowing your identity is in Christ.

Day 14

Yet to all who did receive him, to those who believed in his name, he gave the right to become children of God.

—John 1:12

Satan whispers many lies about our identity.

1. I am what I have or do not have.

   There are great people who have a lot, and great number of people who have nothing. There are also terrible people who have a lot and terrible people who have nothing. What if you lost all of your possession tomorrow? Would that change who you are? No.

2. I am what I do or do not do.

   There is going to come a day when you can't do what you used to do. You're not always going to be able to play sports or cheer. So, if you had to quit playing a sport tomorrow, would that change who you are? No.

3. I am how many likes I get on social media.

   Christian rapper Lecrae said, "If you live for people's acceptance, you'll die from their rejection." There are people who will post at certain times during the day because they say more people will like their post. If you think about that, you may be trying to find your identity in how many likes you get. If you don't get one hundred likes, is your identity changed? No.

4. I am what others say or think about me.

How many of us have ever judged someone only to find out your judgment was wrong? We all have. Maybe that person is just having a bad day. They seem like a jerk, but in reality they are the nicest person you'll ever know.

Our identity does not come from what we do or what others say about us; it comes from who God says we are. Only the Creator can speak into the created.

Your identity is the most important thing about you because you operate out of your identity. If you are in Christ, then you are a child of God. As children of God, God speaks identity into us, and out of that identity we are able to obey.

Being a child of God means you are loved, accepted, and have a purpose.

As children represent their parents, God calls us to represent him to the world around us. That is our purpose. We should pattern our lives after Jesus and do everything in a way that points others to God.

Pastor Paul Tripp said, "When you bask in your identity in Christ, you're free of the craziness of looking for identity in people and places where it can't be found." You no longer have to go and look for acceptance in the world because you have been accepted by the loving Father. The world will never be able to give you the identity that you are looking for. Will you bask in the identity that is yours in Christ? Will you remember that you are a child of God and loved by Him?

Why does the world compete for our identity to be found in it rather than in Jesus Christ?

What does it mean to be a child of God? How is that different from being a child of your parents?

What does John 1:12 mean to you?

Day 15

For we know that our old self was crucified with him so that the body ruled by sin might be done away with, that we should no longer be slaves to sin.

—Romans 6:6

Have you ever switched schools? Maybe your family moved to another town or you transitioned from middle school to high school. My family moved to another town after my sophomore year in high school, and I remember how scared I was to be going to a new school as a junior, knowing no one. More importantly no one knew me . . . or the old me, that is. I got excited when I realized I had the chance to form and present a new me. I had the opportunity to change my identity—who I was, what I looked like, how I acted, and how I dressed before I met my new classmates. I could now be whoever I wanted to be at my new school because I was able leave behind the old me at my previous school.

Think of Romans 6:6. The point of this passage is that, when we surrender our life to Jesus and accept Him as our Lord and Savior, our old self is dead and gone. Our old identity of sin has been eliminated because of what Jesus did on the Cross. It's a new beginning. It's a fresh start. The slate has been wiped clean, and we are now a new creation in Jesus.

If you are a Christian, your old self was as a lost person separated from God. Our old self was based on the sinful desires of our heart. Our new self is forgiven of that sin and the sins to come. We have been justified and cleared of any wrongdoing in the eyes of God. We have been set free!

The acceptance of Jesus as our Lord and Savior and the surrendering of our old self to the One crucified removes the stain and darkness of sin in our lives. It also brings forward His clean and pure light that reveals our new standing with God. Just as I was able to leave my old self at my old school, our old identity is now gone. Our new identity has now come, which brings with it the blessings of love, mercy, and forgiveness.

This new identity we take on is no longer a slave to sin. Sin was once our master and the ruler of our life. Sin consumed every part of who we were. So while God pursued after us and sent His Son to die on the Cross in our place, our sin took us further and further away from Him. But once you have given your life to Jesus as your Lord and Savior, then sin should no longer have a hold on you because it definitely does not have a hold on your soul or eternity. Jesus now holds that!

What do you want to be? What do you want to leave behind? As a Christian your identity is no longer as a child of sin. You are now a child of God. Will you live as someone who is defined by their old self and ways or will you live as someone who has been completely transformed by Jesus?

What have you left behind in your old identity?

How does your life reflect that you are now a child of God?

What does Romans 6:6 mean to you?

Day 16

But you are a chosen people, a royal priesthood,
a holy nation, God's special possession, that you
may declare the praises of Him who called you
out of darkness into His wonderful light.

—1 Peter 2:9

Is your identity given or chosen? The answer is . . . yes.
From the time you were born you had an identity. This
identity is based on who your parents are, what race you
are, where you live, what school you attend, and where or if
you attend church. These are identity markers you had no
control over. For the early stages of your life all your decisions are made for you. So part of who you are has been
given to you. But now . . .

You are not a child anymore. As you get older, you begin
to form your own thoughts. Decisions are made based on
what you have learned from your family and friends and
from your own desires. So . . . what will your identity be?

For many people they associate their identity with being
accepted. They think, "If I am the right person I will be
accepted." Be honest . . . you want to be accepted. Everyone wants to be accepted. That's part of human nature. God
didn't create us to be alone. In Genesis 1:26 when God said,
"Let us make mankind in our image," He set the stage for

community—the Father, Son, and Holy Spirit . . . and you! So being alone isn't part of God's plan for you. Which brings us to a big question. Who will you be?

Today in the insta-book-snap-tweet world you see people turning to social media to find what is acceptable and what isn't acceptable. In fact, 3.2 billion images are posted on social media daily, and these images shape our view of the world. These images are highlights of people's lives— not everyday reality. This is our attempt to choose who we are, but what if our identity is based on who chooses us?

For those that choose to become part of God's kingdom, it is important to know that He has chosen you first! Yes, you said yes to Him, but only because He placed a call on your heart. The world has always and will always try to dictate what your image is, but your true image is more than what accessories you put on yourself. It's what's inside you.

God has created you in His image . . . you are chosen . . . you are His. Your identity is in Christ. Now that is post worthy!

> What does image have to do with our identity?
>
> If we are created in the image of God, how should that impact our identity?
>
> What does 1 Peter 2:9 mean to you?

Shame

Day 17

INTRODUCTION TO SHAME

Over the next few days we will get real about our shame and the ability to escape from it. Be set free from the power of shame. *You are free!* Remember, "If the son sets you free, you will be free indeed" (John 8:36).

You may be experiencing shame from a variety of sources. We can feel shame from our families, shame that we are not good enough in school or extracurriculars, shame in our relationships, or even shame for simply not being who we want to be. At the end of the day, our shame is almost always rooted in our own sinfulness. Satan knows how to expose our shame because all it takes on his part is a reminder of what we've done. Have you ever done something that you aren't proud of and been reminded of it months later? In that moment, it may even feel as though it has just happened. Your palms get sweaty, your face feels flushed, and your heart even begins a quick and familiar beat of "Guil-ty, Guil-ty, Guil-ty."

Why is it so difficult to regain the courage to push on past this shame? For starters, we often turn inward on ourselves when we are faced with shame. Instead, the next three days are going to challenge you to look to God—who has stopped at nothing to remove us of our shame and reclaim us as His own righteous people. When we begin to trust in His strength, His holiness, and His death on the Cross so that we might not die—the shame of our sin and weakness seems pretty small. Isaiah 50:7 echoes our cry, "But the Sovereign LORD helps me; I will not been disgraced. Therefore I have set my face like flint, and I know I will not be put to shame."

With God as our confidence, we can face shame head on—or as Isaiah puts it, we can set our face like flint! Knowing that God helps us, we know we do not live in disgrace, and we will not be put to shame.

Day 18

Fixing our eyes on Jesus, the pioneer and perfecter of faith. For the joy set before him he endured the cross, scorning its shame, and sat down at the right hand of the throne of God.

—Hebrews 12:2

Shame is everywhere, and it is like the cartoons of old when the saddest character would have a single gloomy storm cloud that followed them wherever they went. Shame defined that character, and it was the lens by which they saw themselves. Not only that, but also how the world saw them as well.

This first moment of shame happened in the garden when Adam and Eve rebelled against God, "Then the eyes of both of them were opened, and they realized they were naked; so they sewed fig leaves together and made coverings for themselves" (Genesis 3:7). Their nakedness was their shame. Instead of reacting with complete repulsion or abandonment, God showed in that moment that the schemes of the enemy to shame His creation would not have to be the final blow. He sacrificed an animal and made them clothing from its pelt. God made a sacrifice to cover their shame.

The same is true for us as believers, whether you are a pastor, schoolteacher, stay-at-home mom, a student, or whatever you are, we are not exempt from the enemy's attempt to shame us. We are constantly told by others and ourselves that the sins we commit decrease our value and damage us beyond redemption. Sin becomes our dark storm cloud.

However, we see that Jesus not only knew about shame but also came to absolve us from any trace of it. Jesus is the only one who was able to confront shame and overcome shame to then release His people from shame. Hebrews 12:2 tells us "For the joy set before him he endured the cross, scorning its shame, and sat down at the right hand of the throne of God." Jesus overcame the penalty of our sin, and not just that. He covered us by His grace so that shame has no place in the life of His followers.

Give glory to God that shame has no hold on you. Jesus' blood has already covered it. We have the opportunity today to be light in a world of people who think their dark cloud of shame is too heavy and too regretful for Jesus to cover. Jesus' sacrifice on the Cross covered our shame.

In what way has shame been a part of your daily life?

How might we identify with the shame Adam and Eve felt in the garden?

What does Hebrews 12:2 mean to you?

Day 19

At that time I will deal with all who oppressed you. I will rescue the lame; I will gather the exiles. I will give them praise and honor in every land where they have suffered shame.

—Zephaniah 3:19

When I think of shame, the words of a favorite teacher play repeatedly in my mind. He regularly addresses student mistakes with the words, "I like you! You are a sinner just like me. That means we can be friends and help each other!" Instead of denying our mistake or letting it define us, he approaches the problem of shame with a hopeful attitude, knowing that it has already been overcome.

Unfortunately, we will encounter teachers, bosses, and even friends who do not embrace the shared shame we all experience. Instead they will use our mistakes and sins to point us back to the shame of our former life. I don't know about you, but before the Holy Spirit began working on my heart, I found a lot of joy in evil things. Even thinking about it now reminds me of how shameful my thoughts and actions were. To make matters worse, shame did not leave me alone when I came to Christ. It is like a lion, waiting for me to mess up so it can try to resurrect who I was before Christ.

In Zephaniah 3 God says shame impacts us all. Who among us has not experienced mental or physical strife that we cannot overcome? Who has not felt the loneliness of being a social outcast? Anytime I've been confronted by shame, it has attacked me in one of these two areas. It reminds me that I am weak—both physically and mentally. It knows that others will constantly try to expose my faults, because they really just want to hide their own. When I imagine handling all of this disappointment and shame on my own, I see an impossible and hopeless life . . . but God has a different plan for us!

Zephaniah 3:19 says the Lord will save the lame, and gather the exiles. It promises that this shame will be transformed into praise! No longer will our enemies attempt to push us back into who we were before Christ, but they will rejoice for who we have become in Christ! Imagine a life that acknowledges shame as something God has already overcome and not something that defines who we are. That is the life of freedom that God offers us in the death and resurrection of Jesus Christ!

How does shame impact our ability to have relationship with others?

Why is it important that Christ took on our shame at the Cross?

What does Zephaniah 3:19 mean to you?

Day 20

As Scripture says, "Anyone who believes in him will never be put to shame."

—Romans 10:11

Shame is a byproduct of wrong decisions. We experience shame when we do things that go against what we know to be right. Look at the first people ever created, Adam and Eve. They experienced shame when they broke the one rule God gave them. After they ate the fruit, they were overcome with guilt and shame, and these feelings drove them into hiding. They didn't want God to see them or know what they had done.

Why does shame have that effect on us? It's because shame breeds isolation. When we do things or say things we know we shouldn't, our shame tells us to hide what happened. However, hiding eats us from the inside out because isolation opens the door for us to believe lies we were never meant to believe.

Furthermore, shame has the ability to tear apart families and friendships. You don't want them to know what you have done or what you are currently doing, so you don't want to be around them as much. And when you are around them, you are incapable of truly being yourself for fear that they might realize your shortcomings.

Ultimately, the enemy uses shame to convince us we are worthless and broken beyond repair.

But Christ tells a different story.

Jesus tells us there is no condemnation or shame for those who have a personal relationship with Him.

The Bible is full of stories that could have ended in shame because of the decisions of people but instead ended in redemption because of the love of Christ.

Saul became Paul. God declared David was a man after God's heart. Peter denied Jesus, yet Christ still chose him as the rock of the church. Christ reminds us time and time again that He uses broken people, and His grace is available to all, no matter what decisions you have made in life.

If you have a relationship with Jesus, you have a powerful story of redemption, grace, hope, and love. This testimony carries the ability to help those who are hurting, alone, looking for love, and drowning in shame find the one who keeps no record of wrongs. Don't let shame hold you back. Go and share your story. The people around you need to hear it.

How does freedom in Christ allow you to deal rightly with shame?

Does shame make a difference in how you interact with others?

What does Romans 10:11 mean to you?

Conform

Day 21

Introduction to Conform

Have you ever had to reboot your computer or electronic device? It gets stuck, it develops a quirk, or it simply stops working. What do you do? You press the reset button. But most people have never reset their life to get back on track.

Paul describes to us in Romans that we must not conform to this world. When we are conformed, we are like the elephant tied by a rope. When the elephant is young the trainer will tie the elephant to a pole by a rope. The rope is strong enough for the baby elephant, but as the elephant grows, the rope is never strengthened. It is the same rope, but the elephant has conformed to the idea of not being able to break away. So many of you have grown up being conformed to the ideas that have kept you in bondage. I am asking you to press the reset button. You are either conformed by this world or by the Word of God. Paul uses another term, *transformed*, that gives you the key to being reset.

When you are reset by the Word of God you realize we are called to so much more than we believe. First Corinthians 2:14 gives the key to being transformed by the Word of God. When the Bible is in your life, you are able to have discernment. You look at life through a different set of lenses. Life gets purpose. It becomes focused. You realize what you can do, not what you cannot do.

How did Noah get the ark built before rain? How did Joseph rise from slave to second in command? How did Moses tell Pharaoh to let the people go? How did the Israelites cross the Red Sea? How did David defeat Goliath? How did the disciples turn from denying Christ to being martyred for Him? How did Paul transform from being one who persecuted the church to the greatest missionary the world has ever seen? *God.* All had to reset.

Day 22

It teaches us to say "No" to ungodliness and worldly passions, and to live self-controlled, upright and godly lives in this present age.

—Titus 2:12

When you look in the mirror, do you see the you God wants you to see? Or do you see the you that's trying to be something everyone around you wants you to be?

We all have choices each day that move us into who we become. Maybe you are looking for acceptance, and therefore your choices of what you wear, what you listen to, how you talk, and who you hang with are all centered around trying to impress and fit in with a group of people who may or may not even want to accept you, even if you try as hard as possible to be like them.

As a middle school teacher, I see this daily. I see kids who struggle with their identity, choosing to change how they look and how they act in order to try and find a group of people they can claim as "theirs." We all want to be accepted. Nobody wants to shuffle through life running solo and not having a wingman or two . . . or ten. But, if we are conforming to the image of others and their opinions and not choosing to conform to the image of Christ, then the friends we think we are gaining are not really friends at all.

God created us for relationship with Him, and therefore we all have a yearning inside of us that craves relationships, acceptance, and a desire to be linked to others to help us enjoy life and find meaning in and from it. But when it comes to relationships with others, it can be a very tricky deal if we don't see and understand who we are and whose we are. If we are not careful in guarding our hearts and choosing friends wisely, then we are vulnerable to conforming in our patterns of behavior and life to fit what those around us are doing. Our focus can become acceptance from others over the truth of who God created us to be.

Our life choices should always be centered around God's will, truth, and what He desires of us. In today's society, especially in the middle school and high school world, if you whole-heartedly choose Jesus, you are going to stick out. Your actions and choices will not resemble the majority decision.

But I challenge you in understanding this: standing alone in Christ versus conforming to the masses takes way more bravery and strength and, most importantly, allows you the opportunity to grow daily into the kingdom warrior God wants you to be. Go be a light for Jesus!

What happens when we conform to the world rather than the image of Christ?

What does it look like when someone conforms to the ways of Christ?

What does Titus 2:12 mean to you?

Day 23

Do not conform to the pattern of this world, but be transformed by the renewing of your mind. Then you will be able to test and approve what God's will is—his good, pleasing and perfect will.

—Romans 12:2

For it is written: "Be holy, because I am holy."

—1 Peter 1:16

Conformity sounds like an old-fashioned tradition that churches still try to incorporate because it is something we have always done, right? You probably have also wondered how else you are supposed to reach your lost, unsaved friends if you're not trying to fit in with them and conform to their likes and interests. It's just easier to follow everyone else than try to stand up for what you say you believe!

First, it is important to understand why people take the easy way out. Lack of motivation, fear of the unknown, and low self-esteem drives us to just want to give up. To sum it up, it depends on our mood as to how we will respond to situations. It reminds me of a chameleon. Most believe the chameleon changes colors to avoid predators, which is not entirely false. However, chameleons are quite fast and can escape quickly if they want to. They actually change colors based on their moods. Anger, regulating their body temperature, and attracting mates are just a few of the moods that affect their body color. We do the same thing when we allow our fears and limitations to direct our paths instead of allowing the Holy Spirit to guide us. We switch back and forth and "change colors" based on how our attitude is that day, and we just end up blending into whatever background we find ourselves surrounded by in that moment.

Romans 12:2 tells us to be transformed. In other words, be changed, be different from the world. When we choose to be just like everyone else, we limit our own personal growth not just spiritually but emotionally and physically as well. We lose out on what we can achieve in God and confine our goals to the standard of everyone else.

How can we avoid falling into the trap of conformity? First Peter 1:16 says to *be holy!* In order to clearly see God's will and plan for our lives, we must strive to be like Him. You cannot be like God unless you first have a relationship with God and have accepted Him as the one true God. Then as your relationship grows, the only way to learn to be more like Him is to spend time with Him reading His Word every day and praying to Him asking for direction and guidance so that He is the one that is influencing our moods and not the world.

When God is the focus of our minds and thoughts, we are no longer afraid to stand out! We no longer try to change our mindset to fit in with the latest fashion or trend.

Instead we take the high road, the more difficult path, opposite of the world. Noam Chomsky stated, "Case by case, we find that conformity is the easy way." Instead of choosing to do the bare minimum, why not choose to be different and prove to the world that being godly and holy is a far greater reward that will last an eternity instead of just a moment.

Why are our feelings and desires important when it comes to conforming to the world?

What are some areas that you are working to conform to the image of Christ rather than the world?

What does Romans 12:2 mean to you?

Day 24

Dear friends, do not be surprised at the fiery ordeal that has come on to you to test you, as though something strange were happening to you. But rejoice inasmuch as you participate in the sufferings of Christ, so that you may be overjoyed when his glory is revealed. If you are insulted because of the name of Christ, you are blessed, for the Spirit of glory and of God rests on you. . . . However if you suffer as a Christian, do not be ashamed, but praise God that you bear that name.

—1 Peter 4:12–16

Jesus Christ is the most revolutionary figure in the history of the world. I often remark that His story is so integral to history that we literally changed from BC to AD to mark the historic event of His birth. That leaves us begging the question, why is so much of our focus, as Christians, on conformity? In a day when so many are searching for more, searching to fill that gap in their life from where they are to where they want to be, I believe God is calling us out of our conformity and compromise so we may live lives devoted to making His name known through our actions, our words, and our life as a whole.

According to Scripture, worldly conformity hurts our walk with God. Romans 12:2 says, "Do not conform to the pattern of this world, but be transformed by the renewing of your mind. Then you will be able to test and approve what God's will is—his good, pleasing, and perfect will." Jesus did not come for behavior modification; He did not come to suppress our desires and give us self-help for how to fight them. He came to give us a new desire and relationship with Him. Conformity to the world places us at a distance from Him, leading us to try and face our own temptations and struggles with human will and emotions. Often even wondering what is right and what is wrong. In an age when so many question norms and tradition, God gives us a blueprint for discerning what we should pursue through transformation of our minds to pursuing His will and His way. We follow His will not out of some necessity but out of the privilege of being in relationship with Him (John 14:15).

This can be a scary thought. It is so easy to place ourselves in a position where we simply go through the motions of everyday life with friends and family while never really living out the call God has placed on us. For some, doing so would mean we lose friends, family, and opportunities. A scary thought, but the fear of suffering can never outweigh the faith we have in the risen Savior.

First Peter 4:12–16 reminds us Christ understood what we would face. He understood the temptations we would have and the struggles would face as His followers. But He has still called us to live boldly and daringly. To be salt and light, adding taste to a bland life and light to the darkness in the world (Matthew 5:13–16). To do anything different runs the risk of living a life short of the calling He has placed on us and an unfinished race before us. We are meant to live revolutionary lives that change futures and brighten history. The hands and feet of Jesus cannot be like those of the world! That just won't suffice for His kingdom.

When we think of renewing our minds, how will that combat our conformity to the world?

In what areas are you conformed to the world, and how will you turn your focus back to Christ?

What does 1 Peter 4:12–16 mean to you?

Secure

Day 25

Introduction to Secure

I got the email, and my mind went racing. I was being accused of doing something I knew I had not done, watching things I knew I had not watched, and being offered a ransom in order to not make my proposed indiscretion public. The email contained my username and password that I had used often, and now it was the only proof that I had done something wrong.

After a few moments, reality started to set in about this situation. A hacker had stolen my information from a business website and now was trolling to see who he or she could extort money from. I knew I was innocent of what I was being accused, but for a moment it shook me. In reality, what should really shake me is that the website was not secure. The security had been breached, and my trust for that website would never be the same. In fact, this seems to be a growing issue. In the first six months of 2019, 3,800 public breaches were reported impacting an amazing 4.1 billion records worldwide. Where can anyone find anything that is really secure?

I am so glad you asked! According to Scripture we are secure in Christ. He doesn't play games, He doesn't have a breach, and He doesn't have a system that can be hacked. He is secure. In John 10:28, Jesus says, "I give them eternal life, and they will never perish; no one will snatch them out of my hand." Think about this . . . He will never allow anyone or anything to snatch you out of His hand.

How secure is Christ? He is more secure than a website, a safety deposit box, Snapchat, or Instagram. He is *secure!* Do not walk in fear or dismay. Walk in confidence that you are secure in Christ. Here is what I have found: when you are totally secure in Christ, you are not concerned about what others are saying or thinking.

You may be asking, what about when I thought someone was extorting me? Admittedly, for a second, my heart skipped a beat. However, I found my strength not in what someone was saying about what I had done but in *truth.* When the world starts to threaten you and accuse you of things, do not sweat it. He has you in His hand. He has it all worked out.

These next three days you will discover the power of being secure in Christ. Thank Christ for what He has done in and through you. Take a few moments right now, before you begin, to realize that Christ has you secure. There is nothing that can touch you.

Day 26

I keep my eyes always on the LORD. With him at my right hand, I will not be shaken.

—Psalm 16:8

In our country today, companies, commercials, technology, and even books attempt to convince us that security can be found within ourselves as individuals. As a matter of fact, most of our society pushes this agenda that you really only can trust in yourself, so do what you want with your time; you are the only place where you will truly find security and contentment.

The problem with this worldview is that it does not take into account things you can't control, like your enemies, depression, anxiety, or illness. Where do you find security when it seems as though your world is crashing down all around you? Do you look to fighting against the flesh? Do you look to a doctor? Do you look to your cell phone or technology? At best, the world offers a false sense of security. David wrote about this in Psalm 16, "I keep my eyes always on the LORD. With him at my right hand, I will not be shaken."

David ran from people because of his fear. He slept with another man's wife to please his flesh. David looked everywhere for world security yet fell short. These worldly offerings left David shaken. *None* of these options were good enough for him, and we should take heed that they are not good enough for us either.

I'm reminded of a story someone shared with me about one of their favorite paintings. It was the results from a painting contest that sought to paint the perfect picture of peace. The painting that won was of a stormy night. The clouds were of the strongest and darkest gray, bearing heavy raindrops. The waves crashed on the rocks at the banks of the sea. Yet if you looked closely enough, you'd see a bird standing calmly upon one of the rocks while the storm brought chaos all around it. Somehow, the bird found security in the storm. One thing is for certain: though the bird could not control the storms of life, it somehow found security in the midst of them.

The challenges you face right now should not lead you to escape the storms of life but should spur you on to discover true security is only found in Christ.

What are some of the ways the world offers a false sense of security?

How can you combat the lies of the world with the truths of Scripture?

What does Psalm 16:8 mean to you?

Day 27

So do not fear, for I am with you; do not be dismayed, for I am your God. I will strengthen you and help you; I will uphold you with my righteous right hand.

—Isaiah! 41:10

Fasten your seat belt . . . Did you remember to set the alarm? . . . Make sure to keep your phone on.

Every day we have to deal with situations to make sure we are physically secure. We do this for ourselves and also those who care about us. Those who love us do everything they can to make sure we are secure and feel safe. It doesn't matter how many times we go somewhere, one of the first things I do when we get in the car is tell my kids, "Fasten your seat belt." I know, I know. Your parents do the same, but sometimes we need to be reminded how secure a seat belt can make you.

What about before you go to bed? Your parents turn out all the lights, lock the doors, and you hear one of your parents say, "Did you set the alarm?" Your parents want to make sure everyone is secure and has a safe night's rest.

It's Friday night, and you are headed out because you have made plans to go hang out with a friend. You are excited and ready to go. Before you leave, Mom and Dad stop you to have *the talk*. "Make sure you drive the speed limit," "Make wise decisions," and "Make sure to keep your phone on."

Why? Why would parents want to remind you of these things? Because they want to make sure you are secure and they love you.

In Isaiah 41 the Lord is reminding His people of this same love. He says to them and to us, in essence, "You are my chosen people. No matter what is going on in creation you are secure because I am with you."

The voice of the Lord has a way of calming all the fears we face, doesn't it? Be reminded today that you do not have to fear anything. The Lord is with you. You are *secure* in Jesus. Go forward today with a *no-fear* living attitude!

How have you witnessed God's security in your life?

Write down a few areas in Scripture where God has kept His people secure.

What does Isaiah 41:10 mean to you?

Day 28

Look to the LORD and His strength; seek his face always

—1 Chronicles 16:11

Remember security blankets? You know, the nasty little blanket you couldn't go more than ten minutes without? You dragged that thing through the mud, wiped your nose with it, and yet, you still wrapped yourself up in it every night as you were falling asleep because, as long as it was next to you, you felt secure.

Whether we realize it or not, most of us still hold fast to our security blankets today. Sure, our current blanket probably isn't full of mysterious-looking stains, but it's just as present. We've simply traded in our blankets for status. We tell ourselves, "If I can just get more money, into this friend group or that organization, then I won't have to worry about anything." We think status can protect us from things like anxiety, loneliness, ridicule, and fear. However, as long as we see security as something we can hold on to, we will never find it.

In fact, true security is not found; rather, it is a state of being. We are not secure when we finally feel like we've got it all together but when we find ourselves in the presence of God.

Simply put, security comes from being hidden in Christ.

When we seek His presence, we find the ability to remain secure in who we are and who Christ is, no matter the current season of life or whatever worldly status we might have obtained.

The presence of God may seem mystical and hard to discover. However, He is always present, and the beautiful promise of God is this: when we seek His presence, we will find Him. The James 4:8 reminds us of this truth by saying, "Come near to God and he will come near to you."

It can seem scary to let go of our security blankets and seek security in His presence, but it is so worth it. Status, and, yes, even those old blankets we used to hold so near to us, will fail us, but the Lord never will. Seek His presence. Find His strength. And ultimately, you will find the security in your life we all long for.

What is something in your life that you need to release in order to fully find your security in Christ?

Why do we find security in the presence of God?

What does 1 Chronicles 16:11 mean to you?

weakness

Day 29

Introduction to Weakness

When I am weak, He is strong. Sounds like a song for children, but it is true for all of us. I am not strong enough to carry the burdens of this life, but He is. I am not smart enough to navigate through this labyrinthian thing called life, but He is. I am not . . . but He is!

The realization of weakness is actually the key to finding your strength. As you have been reading, you have noticed a common theme in this book. We are not what we think; we are what He says we are. We must walk with Christ daily to tap into the strength He offers. Prayer is key to your strength. As we walk through the next few days, ask the Lord for the following four things in your prayer life.

First, ask Him to show you something in His Word by speaking directly to you and your circumstances. It is miraculous that every time I read from God's Word, He speaks to me. Even if I had read the passage a hundred times, He still speaks.

Second, ask Him to search you for anything that isn't pleasing. Ask the Lord to search your heart and life for sin. Stay clean and pure before Him. A friend will send me a text from time to time and it simply says, "Stay clean and close." The meaning is simple: stay clean before God.

Third, ask Him to shape you today. Ask the Lord to mold you into His image and allow you to become the leader He wants you to become. This is the mindset of the disciple. It isn't what the student desires but rather the teacher. Learn to follow after His desires, not yours.

Finally, ask Him to supply your needs. Sometimes we have not because we ask not. Be ready to do what He says for you to do.

Sometimes we are weak, not because of what we do not have but because we have the wrong thing in our lives. If you have toxic messages pouring into your life, you will never be strong. As a follower of Christ, get rid of the toxicants of society, and stay close to Christ. When you do, you realize, yes, I am weak, but when I am weak, He is strong!

Day 30

For the flesh desires what is contrary to the Spirit, and the Spirit what is contrary to the flesh. They are in conflict with each other, so that you are not to do whatever you want.

—Galatians 5:17

In Galatians 5, we are given a very simple description from the writer, Paul, in how to avoid sin and deny what evil has to offer. Verse 16 states, "So I say, walk by the Spirit, and you will not gratify the desires of the flesh." Easy, right? Ha! Not at all! So often we see temptation around us, and whether you are long-term believer, you just made a life changing decision to receive Christ last week, or you have no faith background, we all find ourselves giving in to the temptation.

Was that okay to do? Will Christ forgive me? Why am I a bad person? No way my parents can know about this! All of these thoughts begin to pop into our heads. We have sinned, and now we feel the burden of being weak. This is what happens when we see the sin of this world and how it impacts us. The weaknesses people identify in us and the guilt we take on as a result begin to weigh us down. Before we go even further, everyone should know that we all have felt this. You are not the first or last person to find themselves in this place.

The best answer to see around and past our weaknesses is to simply submit them to the Lord. I know this sounds like a cliché church answer that you don't want to find in a devotional, but the power of God is a very real answer. When we focus on Christ and consistently pursue Him, He has the power to not only remove those weaknesses that we identify in but also to alter our desires. When we give God control, we begin to see the fruits mentioned in verse 22 make themselves evident in our everyday lives. We can find joy and peace and love and so much more through a change that cannot be described by words on a page. As Paul mentions twice in this passage, there is no law to restrict what God can achieve. God goes beyond any man's comprehension, and when we switch our focus from a sin-filled identity of what has happened in the past to a life-giving identity as a child of God, our guilt is removed and our weaknesses are redefined and forgotten as we focus on new desires and peace only found in Christ.

Take time today to submit your burdens and weaknesses to God. Let Him into your quiet time today and allow God to start altering your desires to be more aligned with His. Find your identity in the power of God and not in the weakness of man.

What does it feel like to be weak against sin?

How can we find strength in God?

What does Galatians 5:16–26 mean to you?

Day 31

Then the man said, "Your name will no longer
be Jacob, but Israel, because you have struggled
with God and with humans and have overcome."

—Genesis 32:28

Sin is what separated us from God in the beginning.
But praise be to His name, who has overcome death in
order that we might be saved, that we might be given a new
identity, that we might be given a new life and a new name.
Genesis 32:22–32 paints a beautiful example of what the
Lord can do with us when we devote ourselves to Him.

Before Jacob had this supernatural experience, he had
been fearful of facing the conflict with his brother Esau.
At one point he goes to the Lord, asking for His guidance
and assistance in approaching this matter. Yet, in his lack
of faith and his suffocating pride, he takes matters into his
own hands and tries to send Esau gifts, hoping they would
release some of the tension. When we pursue our own
agenda because of our lack of faith in God, we neglect that
He is who He says He is—a sovereign and loving God!

So, as the story goes, Jacob encounters a man, and they
begin wrestling. In the middle of their wrestling match the
man recognizes Jacob is not giving up. However, given that
Jacob is a man filled with pride and fear, we would expect

for him to concede or run away. The man reaches over and touches Jacob's hip, knocking it clean out of socket. Can you imagine the pain Jacob began to feel? How do you think Jacob responded to the pain he was feeling? Just like anyone else would, we can imagine that as soon as his hip was touched and put out of place, he grabbed on to the man with the hope of making the fall feel easier on his already damaged body. We must understand that it is when we recognize our weakness and need that we must respond by clinging on the Lord for His help and guidance. Imagine Jacob's surprise when he realized it was indeed God who he had been clinging onto during the fight! This story paints a physical picture of our very real need to cease our wrestling with God and instead cling to Him! It was after this encounter that Jacob was given a new name and identity—Israel.

God began to use him as a tool for the expansion of His kingdom. Where are you currently placing your trust? Are you relying on the Lord and holding fast to His promises? Or are you relying on yourself and your ability to do what only God can do? It is when we recognize our need for Him that we must remain in Him, in His Word, relying on His truth. Live in such a way that you cling to the Lord!

Why do our weaknesses scare us?

What are some similarities between this story of Jacob and your life?

What does Genesis 32:22–32 mean to you?

Day 32

My flesh and my heart may fail, but God is the
strength of my heart and my portion forever.

—Psalm 73:26

My favorite icebreaker question is, "If you could have
any superpower, what would it be?" When you ask
this question, you can learn a lot about about where people
see their weaknesses and long for superhero-like strength.
Some of us wish to fly so that we can escape danger and
see the world. Others wish for the ability to read minds so
they would never get caught in an awkward social situation
again. Most commonly, our new friends wish for invincibil-
ity—because the truth is, humans are incredibly fragile.

When I read Psalm 73:26, I'm reminded that I am not
entitled to a stress-free life or a body that comes without
weakness. When humanity left the garden, we entered a
world tainted with sin and fallenness. Danger is prevalent
all around us, and although we would like to be conquerors,
we are powerless. That is where God comes in.

We often encounter God most in our weaknesses. Just
as Paul says in 2 Corinthians 12:9, the weaknesses we have
are God's tools to show the world just how strong He is.
The world will see your weaknesses. But when God is the
strength of our heart and our portion forever, the world

is taken by surprise at how mighty the Lord must be to use our weaknesses for good! Imagine a time in your life when you were disappointed in your lack of abilities. For example, you may not be the most gifted in walking up to a stranger and sharing your faith. However, maybe you went with your church on a mission trip and found yourself in the group that decides to do a little door-to-door evangelism. It sounds terrifying to do something you aren't good at, especially when you are called to do it for the kingdom of God. In these moments, you are very aware that your strengths are not going to cut it.

But don't give up quite yet. Although you are weak, you have faith in a very big and powerful God! Though our flesh and heart may fail, the Lord is our strength in weakness. That is pretty incredible! If you find yourself in a situation like the one mentioned, do not run away in fear. Instead, dig deeper into faith that God is the giver of strength, and just watch what He will do in your life!

Where in the Bible have you seen God use the weakest people to make the biggest changes in the world?

What does it say about God that He chooses to glorify Himself in our weaknesses as well as our strengths?

What does Psalm 73:26 mean to you?

Found

Day 33

INTRODUCTION TO FOUND

The movie, *Raiders of the Lost Ark*, is about explorers looking for the ark of the covenant. It depicts the travels and predicaments of Indiana Jones as he frantically searches to beat his opposition to the treasure. It allows us to relate to the idea of searching for something so valuable that you would do anything to be successful in your search. He didn't give up. He didn't give in. He relentlessly pursued.

Have you ever lost something so precious that you began a pursuit? Forsaking everything else, you pursued that which was valuable to you. If you found that item, do you remember the joy? The excitement and relief—both emotions growing into ecstatic joy? These next three days are intended to bring you back to the excitement of being found. You will discover the one who is passionate about you, the attributes of those who are found, and the joy of being under His authority.

In Luke 15 we have an entire chapter of how passionately our God pursues us. He doesn't give up. He doesn't give in. He relentlessly pursues. The first illustration is that of a sheep. There are ninety-nine perfectly fine sheep. They obey. They are safe. However, the Good Shepherd leaves the ninety-nine for the one that is lost. Why? Why would He leave the majority for one who was lost?

Allow me to give you a perspective as a parent. I have two incredible children. If I lose one in the supermarket or store, I don't think that everything is okay because I still have the other one safe. No. The store will be turned upside down in relentless pursuit for the lost child. Why? Because that child is mine. Now, I do not know about your earthly family. I do know your Heavenly Father loves you and has an incredible plan for you. He will not give up. He will not give in. He relentlessly pursues.

The second illustration in Luke 15 is that of a coin. Jesus gives us this illustration so we can understand that our God looks long and hard for us, and that He rejoices over us being found. In this parable the woman basically tells those around, "Celebrate with me, I have found that which was lost!" If heaven celebrates over one being found, why shouldn't we? If you know Jesus personally, you should rejoice that you were lost but now found!

Rejoice that you have been found. God is passionate about you. Don't try to strive for anything over these next three days. Rest. Rejoice. He is for you!

Day 34

Great is the Lord's anger that burns against us because those who have gone before us have not obeyed the words of this book; they have not acted in accordance with all that is written there concerning us.

—2 Kings 22:13

In 2 Kings 22:8–13, while the Temple is being rebuilt, the high priest finds the Book of the Law (Word of God). The Book of the Law had been misplaced during the destruction and reconstruction of the Temple. When the Word was found, the priest read it to the king, and the Book brought the king to his knees. The question I ask you today is: how close are you to losing the Word of God on your life?

We are one of the most informed cultures on the planet. We have the world at our fingertips. Many, if not most of us, have the Word of God on our phones, and we take God's Word wherever we go. But how often do we open the app and take time to hear from God? Even though the Bible may not be lost, it may be hidden in our phone. We hide it by placing other apps we use more often in front. The danger of hiding the Bible is that it gets lost in our daily lives. We go to sleep with intentions to spend time with God in the morning, but our alarms go off, and we hit snooze. We get ready for school and take time to check our messages but forget to read the verse of the day. We go to bed, expecting to spend the final minutes of our night reading the goodness of Scripture but end up scrolling and liking the latest picture collage from someone's birthday.

Today, the challenge is simple, make time with God a priority. Block out distractions, set reminders, and find the Bible app. Bring it to your opening screen so every time you open your phone you are reminded to spend time with the Jesus who gave you everlasting life!

Luke 11:28 reminds us, "He replied, "Blessed rather are those who hear the word of God and obey it."

> When you find new or unfamiliar stories in the Bible during your quiet time, how do you respond?
>
> What are some practical ways for you to make time with God a priority in your life?
>
> What does 2 Kings 22:8–13 mean to you?

Day 35

But God demonstrates his own love for us in this:
While we were still sinners, Christ died for us.

—Romans 5:8

"1-2-3, ready or not, here I come." What a thrilling memory of jitters and excitement this game from childhood stirs. It was always fun to be the last one found in the game of hide-and-seek. I remember holding my breath as the seeker got close, not wanting to give any clue that I was hiding nearby. And then came the screams as both of us, the hider and the seeker, locked eyes knowing the game was over and all had been found.

In real life, it's not a game. But it's a real need all of us crave. Lostness is continually swirling around each of us. We all are on a hunt to find things: directions, perfect relationships, improved resources, more control, happiness, freedom, a sense of belonging, more time, higher position, more accolades . . . the list seems endless and exhausting until the ultimate prize of salvation is found!

We are all lost until the moment of salvation happens for us. Then we are found, and the exhausting search ends with an amazing peace and joy that engulfs us with the love of Jesus Christ. "But God demonstrates his own love for us in this: While we were still sinners, Christ died for us"

(Romans 5:8). What a big find is Jesus! God's gift of salvation for each of us is mind-blowing.

And the Word is clear that Jesus Christ wants everyone who is lost to be found. In Luke 15 Jesus gives us a parable of the joy that comes from turning from lost to found. He emphasized it with three stories. The first story is about one lost sheep and the celebration from friends and family over it being found. Story number two describes a woman who loses one of her silver coins, and when it is found she calls her friends to celebrate with her. The third story tells us about a son who left home. His family felt he was gone and lost forever. Then one day the son's father saw him coming home, and he was so excited he put together a feast and grand celebration because his lost son had been found.

Why would Jesus give us these special parables? Because Jesus does not want any one of us lost. He wants all of us to be found.

Like the words in the song, "Amazing Grace." When we are found, we finally are able to see. When we see him, lock eyes with him, we too can squeal with delight that the exhausting hunt is over. "In the same way, I tell you, there is rejoicing in the presence of the angels of God over one sinner who repents" (Luke 15:10).

Be the one who is found!

What is the response in each of the parables mentioned when the lost are found?

How can you rejoice in being found by God?

What does Romans 5:8 mean to you?

Day 36

Not only is this so, but we also boast in God through our Lord Jesus Christ, through whom we have now received reconciliation.

—Romans 5:11

It's a terrifying thing to be lost. But you never really know you're lost until you realize you're lacking something. I can remember being lost in a department store as a child and not becoming worried until I noticed my mother wasn't around. What was it that concerned me? I was having fun running between clothes racks and hiding just moments before. What changed? For all I knew, in my five-year-old mind, I was never going to see her again! Danger was everywhere. Who would take care of me, where would I sleep, and what would I eat? My anxiety went from zero to one hundred in the blink of an eye!

It's funny how our minds work in times of distress, but do you really believe that when I was five years old, in that brief moment of being lost, I thought about my daily needs? Of course not. I just wanted my mom! But that's exactly what we're learning here. We often never realize our lostness until we see what's no longer a part of our lives. On a larger lifelong scale, we attempt to fill our days with joys and blessings that mask our lostness or our need to be found. We're perfectly content running around between clothes racks and hiding. In our busy lives we never seem to grasp the eternal need of being found. We never seem to have that moment of stopping and realizing that "I am lacking something" as I did in that department store.

But here's how God has provided the way to be found.

God so loved the world to the point that He was willing to give up His Son on the Cross. The death of Christ on the Cross for you and me displays His immeasurable love for sinners. That love not only took on the sin of an unreceptive world but also showed that Christ was willing to suffer hostility and rejection for a lost people. And now the Holy Spirit is the one who brings to the sinner's mind the immense love displayed on the Cross, making the death of Jesus the ultimate act of making those who are lost found!

You see, when I realized I was lost in that department store, I saw my need for my mother. But just moments before, I wandered off by myself, thinking I could operate outside of her protection. It wasn't until I realized how much I depended on her and loved her that I searched for her. God knows that, on our own, we are not a people who will search for Him or find Him; thus, He provided a way to be found through His Son Jesus Christ. You need only realize that you are lacking something eternal and trust in Jesus Christ for salvation.

Do you believe you are lost or found?

How has feeling apart from God in the past made you cry out for His presence?

What does Romans 5:11 mean to you?

Hidden

Introduction to Hidden

I will never forget the first time I saw it. How did I not think of it? As a dad with a daughter, I had to take her to this concert. It was the latest tween sensation that could fill an arena with young, screaming girls. Everyone was given a bracelet that looked like a cheap smart watch. It was bulky, but since everyone else was wearing one, we did also.

The lights went down, the screams came out, and the star took the stage. All of a sudden, she screamed something like, "Hit it!" and then it happened. Every bracelet began a personal light show that lit up the room. When they all lit up with synchronicity, the bracelets created pictures and made designs that kept this dad intrigued. Here is the deal . . . when the bracelets were left alone and turned off, they were weird. It was when the bracelets worked together that they made the impact.

When we try to live the Christian life by ourselves or, worse, turned off to the power of Christ, we will wonder if Christ really is who He says He is or can do what His Word says He can do. However, when we are in sync with Him and the Holy Spirit is flowing through us, we discover what an incredible display He has in us.

The world is ready to see Christians hidden in Christ. I have nothing to offer this world in regard to peace, hope, or love. Our churches have nothing to offer this world of themselves. It really doesn't matter what type of programs, brochures, or buildings we may have, the world wants to see Christ displayed through us. It *needs* to see Christ displayed through us.

This week we will walk through being hidden in Christ, allowing Him to work through us, in us, and make us a display for the world to be amazed! Colossians 3:3 says, "For you died, and your life is now hidden with Christ in God." When we die, we find life! It is not a physical death Paul is referring to but a spiritual death. A surrender of one's will to Christ.

If you are hidden in Christ, who will the world see? Who will your friend's notice? They will notice Christ. This week let's focus on not being "known" by our friends but being hidden in Christ!

Day 38

There is nothing concealed that will not be disclosed, or hidden that will not be made known.

—Luke 12:2

We all see life through different lenses. Our past makes us think we all have the same finish line but not the same starting line. Good or bad, there are pieces of our stories we cannot wait to share and others we hope no one finds out about. Luke 12:2 finds itself sandwiched between a frontstage life and a backstage life. Whether you believe it or not, we all live our lives in both of these areas.

This passage amplifies that our past, present, and future decisions will always find themselves entering the frontstage of our life at some point. Just imagine an entire theatre filled with your friends and family, and you are on stage in a chair with a giant screen behind you. The movie for the evening is every word, emotion, and act you have ever done in private. The experiences that were covered up have now become known to all.

A life lived in secret is a life lived in fear. Desperate for help, wholeness, and fulfillment, our soul's thirst cannot be quenched behind locked doors, secret texts, or cleared histories. But there's good news. God wants us to fight our secret battles through the lens of His public victory for you and me. The Word tells us to flee from sin, but it also calls us to pursue Him with other believers. Hidden secrets are the seventeen-foot-high and five-foot-thick concrete walls that divide God's purpose from our sinful desires. Although this may seem like a barrier that says, "No one will ever know," walls even as thick as these are no match for God. Ask those who lived in the reality of Joshua 6. When the walls of Jericho fell to allow God's people to enter the Promised Land, what once was a barrier became stepping-stones to a new destination and fulfillment of the promise of God. God's promise is that He will never leave you nor forsake you, so we may boldly say with confidence the Lord is my Shepherd, whom shall I fear?

Do not live a life of sin covered up with empty worship, but instead come out of hiding and pursue God. Walk with God on a path for all to see!

Are there any hidden things in your life that you haven't surrendered to the Lord?

God already knows our hidden sin. What changes when we go to Him?

What does Luke 12:2 mean to you?

Day 39

And the God of all grace, who called you to his eternal glory in Christ, after you have suffered a little while, will himself restore you and make you strong, firm and steadfast.

—1 Peter 5:10

Have you ever taken the blame for something you did not do? It could have been for something small, like stealing a pencil, or maybe for something bigger, like breaking your neighbor's window while playing baseball. Either way, that feeling is not one we enjoy. It brings out anger and makes us want revenge. Could you imagine being falsely accused of burning down an entire empire and having the people blame you for their hopelessness and homelessness? That is exactly what happened to the Christians who lived in Rome under the emperor Nero. Nero ordered his people to burn down much of Rome. After he burned areas of Rome, the citizens turned on each other and looked for someone to blame. Nero directed all of their hostility and violence to the Christians. Christians were already hated because of their relation and communication with the Jews. Because of this, Christians had to deal with this constant persecution while trying to rebuild their homes.

Peter wrote a letter, with the power of the Holy Spirit, to encourage the Christians. Peter encouraged them not to lose hope or become bitter. He also told them of the spiritual benefits waiting for them if they kept their minds focused on Jesus' return. No matter how tough our lives become, there is always a greater hope. As followers of Jesus, we have the ability to call on Him whenever we need Him. We are able to cry out to Him for strength and reassurance. We are promised eternal life with Him when we are saved, but we are also promised hard times in the here and now.

God allows suffering for our good and His glory. In Romans 8:28 it says, "And we know that all things work together for good to those who love God, to those who are called according to His purpose" (NKJV). It may be hard to understand, especially during dark times, but it proves to be true in every situation. When He allows us to suffer, He gives us opportunities to be a light in this dark and dying world. The Christians in Rome could have acted out in anger and violence, but that would not reflect God. When we go through difficult times, God strengthens our character and glorifies Himself.

So when we are faced with hard or unfair situations, we are called to remember that God is allowing us to go through them. Take time to pray that God will give you understanding and self-control when in the midst of challenging circumstances. If we focus our eyes on Him, He will be glorified even on the toughest days.

Why is it important to be hidden in the Lord when we go through suffering?

How does God glorify Himself in the suffering of His people?

What does 1 Peter 5:10 mean to you?

Day 40

You are the light of the world. A city set on a hill cannot be hidden. Nor do people light a lamp and put it under a basket, but on a stand, and it gives light to all in the house. In the same way, let your light shine before others, so that they may see your good works and give glory to your Father who is in Heaven.

—Matthew 5:14–16 ESV

In children's church we used to sing a song, "This Little Light of Mine." One of the verses says, "Hide it under a bushel? *No!* I'm gonna let it shine." I never really thought a lot about it, but there really is a lot of wisdom embedded in those words we sang as children.

As a Jesus follower, we are called to let our light shine before others.

As we read in Matthew 5:14–16, we let our light shine so others may see Jesus, not for us to receive any recognition. When we accept Jesus Christ we are to put to death our selfish desires and hide ourselves in Him. Our choice to die to self allows us to focus on Jesus and His call on our lives.

Colossians 3:2–3 (ESV) says, "Set your minds on things that are above, not on things that are on earth. For you have died, and your life is hidden with Christ in God."

Following Jesus means people no longer see you. Instead they see you hidden in Christ Jesus. We are to hide ourselves behind Jesus (the Cross) every day. Doing so allows us to live a life full of purpose. We hide our self in Christ so we don't hide our light (relationship with Jesus) from the world.

Jesus followers have a story to tell to this lost and dying world. Are you telling yours? When was the last time you prayed to have a gospel-centered conversation with someone? Opportunities for these conversations are all around us. Are you going to shine yours, or will you hide in fear?

When people look at you, do they see Jesus hidden within your heart?

Hands
And to aspire to live quietly, and to mind your own affairs, and to work with your *hands*, as we instructed you. —1 Thessalonians 4:11 ESV (emphasis added)

Instruct
For whatever was written in former days was written for our *instruction*, that through endurance and through the encouragement of the Scriptures we might have hope. —Romans 15:4 ESV (emphasis added)

Declare
Declare these things; exhort and rebuke with all authority. Let no one disregard you. —Titus 2:15 ESV (emphasis added)

Direct

May the Lord *direct* your hearts to the love of God and to the steadfastness of Christ. —2 Thessalonians 3:5 ESV (emphasis added)

Examine

Examine yourselves, to see whether you are in the faith. Test yourselves. Or do you not realize this about yourselves, that Jesus Christ is in you?—unless indeed you fail to meet the test! —2 Corinthians 13:5 ESV (emphasis added)

Nation

But you are a chosen race, a royal priesthood, a holy *nation*, a people for his own possession, that you may proclaim the excellencies of him who called you out of darkness into his marvelous light. —1 Peter 2:9 ESV (emphasis added)

CONTRIBUTORS

Scott Dawson

Scott has been preaching the gospel since he was a teenager. The ministry that began with simple testimonials and youth rallies has grown into an evangelistic association that reaches across age and denomination in evangelistic efforts to offer a unifying message of hope: the good news of Jesus Christ. Scott makes it a priority to keep his presentations real, innovative, and contemporary. Coming from a broad denominational background, he has a keen understanding of the factors that drive churches apart and strives to focus on the common ground that draws Christians closer together. Scott lives in his hometown of Birmingham, Alabama, with his wife Tarra, son Hunter, and daughter Hope.

Hunter Dawson

Hunter was born and raised in Birmingham, Alabama, and has been involved with the Scott Dawson Evangelical Association (SDEA) since childhood. Since graduating from Samford University last year with a degree in accounting, he has been serving as a financial consultant, leading strategist, and speaker for SDEA. Hunter is married to his high school sweetheart. In his free time, he enjoys all things food and sports. He and his wife Shannon attend Church of the Highlands at the Grandview campus.

Ben Birdsong

Ben serves as the minister of students at Meadow Brook Baptist Church in Birmingham, Alabama. He has served in church and para-church student ministry for more than ten years. Ben has bachelor's degrees in marketing and human resource management from the University of Alabama at Birmingham, a masters of divinity degree from Samford University's Beeson Divinity School, and a doctor of ministry in ministry to emerging generations from Gordon-Conwell Theological Seminary. Ben is married to Liz. He enjoys reading, writing, watching movies, and blogging at www.benbirdsong.com.

Taylor Borders

Taylor enjoys listening to music, playing the guitar, reading books, and spending time with family and friends. He attended Auburn University and earned a degree in human development and family studies, adolescent development. Taylor married his wife Kelsie in August 2011, and they have two sons, Ty and Miles.

Maddie Bowman

Maddie is eighteen years old and a 2019 graduate from Trinity Christian Academy in West Tennessee. She is the daughter of a youth pastor and has been attending Strength to Stand Conferences for as long as she can remember. She became a follower of Christ at the age of thirteen and is involved in ministry at Chapel Hill Baptist Church leading children in worship, along with VBS and camps. She loves musical theatre and anything to do with music and ministry.

Kelly Castleberry

Kelly has started her freshman year at Florida State University. She has a heart for music and a passion for ministry. Kelly is a coffee enthusiast, and in her spare time, she loves reading, writing, watching Netflix, and spending time with her best friend/dog Harper. She is also very appreciative of any corny jokes you may have to share.

Justin Caton

Justin was raised in Jemison, Alabama, and has been working with youth/college age groups since 2007 when he was called into the ministry. Since then, Justin has graduated from the University of Montevallo with a bachelor of science in communication studies and Southwestern Theological Seminary with a master's in theological studies. He is married to Bridget, and they have a son.

Heath Dorning

Heath is the youth minister at Wooley Springs Baptist Church. He is married to Kristin, and they have two sons, Jayden and Hudson. He is currently enrolled in Luther Rice University in biblical and theological studies.

Michael Evans

Michael is the student pastor at Crossroads Baptist Church. He has been a trusted partner and friend to SDEA for many years.

Amber Hardy

Originally from a growing town in Tennessee, Amber moved to Birmingham, Alabama, to begin Beeson Divinity School and earn a master's of divinity. She now considers Birmingham home and loves all the things the area has to offer—hiking, city life, good libraries, and great friends!

Billy Hatley

Billy worked in management for the F. W. Woolworth Co. from 1966–1972. He also served in four churches as pastor for thirty-one years in the state of Alabama. Billy enjoys his faith, family, friends, and sports. Billy is married to his wife Gerrie, and they have one daughter Kari and her husband Todd Burr and two sons Kely and his wife Lassie, Keny and his wife Tracy. Billy and Gerrie also have eight grandchildren.

Scott Huff

Scott is the associate/teaching pastor at Coastal Community Church in Charleston, South Carolina. He and his wife Lori have two beautiful daughters, Carly and Anniston. Scott has a bachelor's degree from Hannibal LaGrange College and a master's of divinity from The Southern Baptist Theological Seminary. Scott was a student pastor for nearly fifteen years and has been a national speaker for more than ten years, including many DNow weekends, worship experiences and events, FUGE, Student Life, and Strength to Stand camps. Scott has a calling on his life to impact the lives of people with the gospel and to lead them to strengthen their faith for glorifying God in an ever-changing world.

Caleb Jones

Caleb graduated from Samford University in December 2017 and has been full time at Strength to Stand since early spring. Caleb claims both Atlanta, Georgia, and Louisville, Kentucky, as home. Caleb has a heart for students to know Jesus and feel accepted. He currently runs our social media, and he is also one of the evangelists on staff. Caleb and his wife Tori attend Christ City Church.

Tori Jones

Tori is a graduate of the University of Georgia and is currently a writer and program consultant for Boosterthon. She is married to Caleb Jones, and they live in Birmingham, Alabama.

Ryan Keaton

Ryan is the associate pastor and minister of students at Lexington, First Baptist Church where has served on staff for the past nine years. He is a prospective doctor of ministry graduate for May 2020 from Mid-America Baptist Theological Seminary and holds an master of divinity from Southeastern Baptist Theological Seminary and a bachelor of arts from Union University. He and his wife Rebecca have been married and serving in ministry together for the past four years.

Dominic Kendall

Dominic is the student pastor at Enon Baptist Church. He is married to Meredith.

Seth King
Seth is the minister to students at First Baptist Church at Decatur. He is a graduate of Samford University and has a heart for service.

Jon Labonte
Jon is the worship pastor at The Well Church. He studied Christian apologetics at Biola University. He is married to Emily, and they have one beautiful daughter.

Tami Lenning
Tami is the director of hospitality and partner relations at SDEA. She has earned an associate of arts degree from Anderson College and attended Furman University to earn a BA in early childhood/elementary education. She met and married the love of her life, Scott Lenning, and they have a son Jonathan who is married to Catherin, and two daughters, Brittany who is married to Tyler, and Scottie who is married to Scott. They have also been blessed with several grandchildren!

Kenny Martin
Kenny is the student minister at West End Baptist Church. Kenny works with students from all over Chilton County and speaks to students all over the country. He is married to Jessica, and they have a son, Barrett.

Joel Morgan
Joel is the college and student pastor at Immanuel Baptist Church. He earned his master's degree from Mid-America Baptist Theological Seminary in 1996. He is married to Rita, and they have four children, Caleb, Eli, Anna Catherine, and Benjamin.

Kristen Oswalt

Kristen is a senior at the University of Alabama majoring in communication. She has volunteered at the Strength to Stand Conferences for the past four years. During the school year, Kristen serves with a student ministry in her hometown of Northport, Alabama. When she gets the chance, Kristen enjoys traveling and being outdoors—anywhere she can admire God's creation from a new perspective and spend time with family and friends.

TJ Phelps

TJ attended college at the Auburn University of Montgomery. His family consists of his wife Ryan and their daughter Lucy. He serves as the student minister at Mineral Springs Baptist Church.

William Roberts

William is in his fourth year at the University of Alabama studying political science and history. He has worked for numerous political candidates across the state of Alabama. He loves a good football game in Bryant Denny Stadium on Saturday night and attending the Tuscaloosa campus of Church of the Highlands on Sunday morning. He is excited for this opportunity to serve a greater purpose and see students impacted with the gospel and never be the same.

Jeremy Shaw

Jeremy is the youth and recreation pastor at Vonore Baptist Church. He has been involved with youth in various capacities, and we are excited God has led him to help develop and mentor our youth and community for Christ. Jeremy and his wife Amanda have two children, Emma Hope and Eli.

Caleb Waid

Caleb is the student pastor at Gardendale First Baptist Church. He earned a master's of arts education from New Orleans Baptist Theological Seminary. He is married to Brittney, and they have three children.

Josh Whitt

Josh is a seventh-grade teacher and coach at Berry Middle School in Hoover, Alabama. He is married to Shannon and they have three kids, Caden, Laura Grace, and Timothy. He and Shannon have been volunteering for Strength to Stand events for several years now. They attend church at Argo Christian Fellowship.

Carson Windle

Carson is the middle school pastor at Olive Baptist Church. He is married to Heather, and they are expecting their first son, Baker Windle.